WAD. £1-20

GW00707276

HIGH TIDE AT PORT ISAAC

The Life and Times of

Warwick Richard Guy
1821 – 1905
by

MONICA WINSTANLEY

c/942·
3710924

LODENEK PRESS

Padstow   Cornwall

CORNWALL
COUNTY LIBRARY

Warwick Richard Guy's signature, taken from a family album, and dated November 18th 1880.

Warwick Richard Guy about 1892.

CONTENTS

ILLUSTRATIONS

PREFACE

A brief history of Port Isaac has already appeared in my 'Story of Port Isaac, Port Gaverne and Port Quin' (Lodenek Press, 1973), but it is of necessity wide ranging and lacking in detail. This present booklet, which concentrates on a century of life in Port Isaac, in no way replaces its predecessor, but rather complements it. Repetition of all but the most essential material has been avoided. In this account particular attention is paid to the everyday life of the community, and in addition to this we trace the life of one man, who perhaps more than any other shaped Victorian Port Isaac.

Yet again I am greatly indebted to the people of the village for their help with this project. I should like to record my thanks for the kindness and hospitality of the following people: Mrs. Bunt of Fore Street, Mr. J. Brown of New Road, Mr. R. Gorman of Church Hill, Mrs. W. Brown of Fore Street, and Mrs. Lobb of Rose Hill. I am especially grateful to Mrs. B. Blake of Tintagel Terrace for her help with the Guy family history. It is an especial pleasure to thank Mrs. S. Sherratt for her tremendous help with this work, and for her patience in sharing so many of her memories of old Port Isaac with me: I should like to dedicate this book to her with my sincere thanks.

I should also like to thank Mr. R. Sloman of Roscarrock Farm, the National Trust, and St. Endellion Parish Council. For photographs I am grateful to Mrs. B. Blake, Mr. R. Gorman, Mr. J. Watt, the Woolf-Greenham Collection (Newquay), the Gillis Collection (Newquay), Mr. F. Ross of Port Gaverne Hotel, and Mr. Jack Ingrey of St. Merryn.

M.W.

INTRODUCTION

This small book looks at Port Isaac at a time when the village was at the height of its importance as a trading port, and enjoying the hey-day of its fishing industry. This is the story of the individuals, the fishermen and their families, the sea captains and the traders who lived and worked in the bustling little nineteenth century community. It is set in the time when the streets resounded with the clatter of horses and carts, and when the smell of pilchards filled the tiny passages and alleyways.

The life of one man seems almost to mirror the changing fortunes of the village: he was Port Isaac's premier entrepreneur, and his name was Warwick Richard Guy. Guy's lifetime in and around Port Isaac spanned the whole of Victoria's reign; indeed in some ways he appears almost a caricature of the Victorian capitalist.

In the years considered here, life was not easy for the people of Port Isaac; for most families it was imperative that everyone worked, including the children, as and when they became old enough. Wages were often poor and housing conditions were barely adequate. Yet, despite the harshness of their lives, one senses that all these people contributed a great deal to the character and undeniable charm of the present-day village.

BEGINNINGS

In the early years of the nineteenth century, the north coast of Cornwall experienced a boom in its fishing industry: so vast were the shoals landed that although the catch might be sold 'almost for nothing', still the share fisherman earned as much as eighteen shillings a week. On September 10th 1802, Warwick Guy of St. Endellion leased out part of his land at Port Gaverne for the erection of new fish cellars to cope with the demands of the growing industry. Soon three other such undertakings had been started in the village, and large cellars were also constructed at the neighbouring villages of Port Isaac and Port Quin. The new century heralded a new era for these ports, and for one local family in particular.

The Guy family were yeomen landowners. In the eighteenth century they worked land at Penmain as well as at Roscarrock, and many early memorials to them can be seen at the churches of St. Minver, St. Endellion, and St.Michael's, Porthilly. The Guy's held Roscarrock Manor for three generations. In 1347 it had been the property of Cornish M.P., John de Roscarrock, and it remained in his family for many centuries. More recently it had belonged to the Earl of Westmorland, and later to a Dr. Mean who sold it to one of the tenants, Warwick Guy. In 1799 Warwick Guy and his kinsman, Jonathan, offered the manor farm and barton for sale by auction, but the family retained the Manor, which paid a modus of £9 in lieu of tithes. In keeping with an ancient custom this money had to be paid at St. Endellion church porch before sunrise on Michaelmas Day. Although Warwick died at the age of 72 in 1819, his leasing out of the land at Port Gaverne marked the start of an association between his family and the port that was to last for a hundred years.

Periodically the fishing failed; for example, during the years 1810-1815, pilchards were exceptionally scarce and costs soared. In 1811 a hogshead of pilchards cost £9, in 1815 £5; but by the mid-twenties the situation had improved, and there were then an estimated 360 fishing seines in Cornwall. (It was estimated that in a good year over 40,000 hogsheads of pilchards were caught in Cornwall: one hogshead equals $4\frac{1}{2}$ cwt.) The parish of St. Endellion was growing. In 1801 it had a population of just 727 (in 146 houses); by 1821 this had risen to 1149, and by 1831 to 1218. When the fishing prospered, so did the villages, and in the eighteen twenties there was a further spate of building in Port Isaac and Port Quin. It was into this relative prosperity, and the security of Roscarrock Manor that Warwick Guy's son, Mark, brought up his own children.

Warwick Richard Guy was born on April 6th 1821. He was

Roscarrock Manor, the home of the Guy family for three generations. The Tudor farmhouse was the home of Nicholas Roscarrock, the Cornish historian and hagiographer.

The porch at St. Endellion Church where before sunrise on Michaelmas Day the £9 modus was paid by Roscarrock Manor.

the second of three sons born to Mark and Jenefer Guy of Roscarrock in St. Endellion. That parish reaches across many
miles of bleak, windswept coastline, and in the spring of 1821
the harshness of the countryside must have seemed to reflect
some of the social inclemency of Georgian Cornwall. Larceny
was punishable by transportation, arson was a capital offence,
and even vagrancy was punished with the treadmill. Twelve
year old children were sent to work as 'stamp' boys in the
mines. There were outbreaks of terrible diseases such as
cholera, and for many of the poor loomed the prospect of the
workhouse.

        The north coast was an isolated, self-dependent district
of obvious remoteness. Although the railways were to reach
into Cornwall in 1859, they were not to come to Camelford and
Port Isaac until the eighteen nineties. Coaching was the main
form of long distance travel, but it was slow (the approved
rate was just thirteen miles an hour), and uncomfortable; the
prices were prohibitive. Even a relatively short journey
could cost a week's wages; for example, the journey from
Launceston to Exeter on the 'Times' coach cost 14 shillings
riding 'inside' and 7 shillings 'outside'. For Port Isaac the
nearest coaching routes passed at Camelford and Wadebridge
(stopping at the King's Arms and Molesworth Arms respectively).
The journey to London took almost three days.

        Around Port Isaac the roads were pitted and bumpy, so
that even riding was not without hazard: in 1837 Elijah
Kellow from Port Isaac was killed near St. Endellion church
when his horse stumbled and threw him into a deep pool of
water by the roadside. With travel so difficult, it is not
surprising that the little communities in the area developed
their own strong senses of identity, and there was little
communication between them. A newspaper report of 1859 speaks
of a woman moving the few miles from St. Endellion into the
neighbouring parish of St. Minver, to conceal the confinement
of her illegitimate child.

        In the valley below Roscarrock Manor was the expanding
village of Port Isaac with some seventy to eighty houses
huddled around its tiny harbour. It was rapidly becoming the
most important place in the parish; and Warwick Richard Guy,
son of a yeoman farmer, was about to make his fortune.

                        THE PORT ISAAC SHIPS

        Warwick Richard's father, Mark, had invested wisely
during the success of the local fisheries. In 1828 he built
a number of cottages at Port Quin; nine years later in March
1837 he paid out a total of £60 at a public auction, and

became the sole owner of the Rashleigh seine at Port Gaverne. But it was not with the fisheries that Warwick Richard was to find his future.

Trade was the new watchword in Victorian Port Isaac. The thriving little community needed goods from outside, as well as a means to export its own produce: the nearby Delabole slate quarry produced some 120 tons of slate daily which required transportation. Along with Trebarwith and Boscastle, Port Isaac and Port Gaverne became trading ports to supply these needs. Elsewhere in Cornwall, shipping was becoming important; in 1869 the first shipments of china clay left Fowey in the 'Rippling Wave'. Warwick Richard Guy moved into the shipping business. By now he was married; his wife, Mary, some five years younger than her husband, was the daughter of James and Elizabeth Stephens. A beautifully scripted page in an old family album records that she was born on February 21st 1826, at half-past nine a.m. Those were days of slow and measured detail. Warwick Richard Guy soon owned his own shipbuilding yard on Roscarrock Hill, but it was rather small and was used mainly for repair and other general work; most of the shipbuilding was undertaken at Port Gaverne. Thomas Mitchell and Thomas May also built ships at Port Isaac and Port Gaverne. The completion of a new vessel was, of course, a time of excitement and celebration; it was common practice for the owner to take his entire family, even small babies, to inspect the new vessel. One day Guy walked over to Port Gaverne to look at a new ship that was being built for him from the salvaged remains of a wreck; thinking that this vessel was bound to be a 'good buy', he enquired the builder's price: suffice it to say that the ship was named 'The Surprise'.

The shipyards and general trade brought welcome employ-ment to Port Isaac, at a time when it was struggling to recover from the 'Hungry Forties'. Journeymen sailors earned about two shillings a day, while the mates who were responsible for the ship's masts and rigging were paid more. The captain of a trader was well paid; his was a job that carried considerable social status and relative affluence. The children of a sea-captain ate beefsteak pasties, whilst those of the fishermen had to make do with bacon and lard ones. One of Guy's captains was Richard Mitchell, who lived at the top of Church Hill in a cottage that he rented from Guy. Mitchell, who was known locally as 'Dandy Dick' on account of his smart clothes, was the master of the 'Bessy Jane' which was the last ship to be built at Guy's yard on Roscarrock Hill. After his retirement Mitchell moved away from Port Isaac to Polruan. Next door to Richard Mitchell's cottage lived another sea-captain called Rowe, and captains Remick, Keat, Couch and Hawke lived in Dolphin Street.

Clearly there was money to be made from shipping, and by the time he was middle-aged Guy was quite prosperous and owned some five or six vessels. But it was a vulnerable business; between 1823 and 1846 some 130 ships were lost along the forty miles of coastline between Land's End and Trevose Head. Even without mishaps at sea, considerable money was needed to maintain a shipping concern. A single repair could cost thirty or forty pounds, and sails and rope were both expensive items; a lower topsail cost nearly £8. It was by no means unheard of for a ship to run at an overall loss for the year. Freight charges were often related to the value of the cargo. In the mid-nineteenth century coal cost 4s.3d per ton, oats 7 shillings per ton and pitwood 3 shillings per ton.

Guy's trading ships are listed in Appendix A. He saw the loss of the 'Volunteer' in 1878 and the 'Surprise' in 1893. Amongst the other locally owned schooners at Port Isaac were two Padstow built vessels: the 'Little Racer' of Mr. J. M. Fishley, and the 'Mary Coad' belonging to Mr. J. G. Coad. But it was not only local ships that traded at the port; one regular visitor was the coal-carrying 'Rifleman' of Bideford.

THE VILLAGE

Guy's investments did not end with the shipping; he also owned property and land in and around Port Isaac. At this time the village consisted of the cottages at the bottom of the valley, close to the fish-cellars, and in Middle Street, Dolphin Street, Church Hill, and Fore Street. There were also a few cottages in Rose Hill, and at one time there was a dwelling above the fish-cellars. Beyond Canadian Terrace were the green fields which stretched over to Port Gaverne.

Warwick Richard Guy had caught the high tide of prosperity at Port Isaac; he had money to invest at a time when wages were cheap and labour plentiful. He soon owned property on Church Hill, in Dolphin Street, and tenements at Trewetha, Homer Park, and Little Trefriock. Perhaps even more importantly, he owned the largest village store. The shop, which is now part of the Slipway Hotel, served as a chandlers as well as a general stores, and from it Guy marketed goods which had been brought in by his own vessels. The shop sold two particularly important commodities, namely coal and salt. Both were shipped in bulk, the coal being stored in cellars under the old Methodist Church, and the salt stored in 14lb. blocks in a cellar of a cottage on Church Hill. Some of the shop's stock had to be brought into the village by horse and cart; the paraffin and oils were brought in in this way. At the end of the eighteen nineties, two gallons of paraffin would have cost 1s.8d.

The Guy family plot (foreground) in St. Endellion churchyard.

The Old Mill at Port Isaac; note the remains of the mill pond in foreground.

Fore Street, Port Isaac. Note the unsurfaced road. The large general stores had been converted from two cottages.

The shop was beautifully kept, with neat rows of
polished wooden drawers and cupboards; a fine selection of
whole cheeses was stocked, and most enticing of all was the
aroma of the freshly ground coffee. Local butter was sold,
but it was expensive, costing 6d a lb. in the summer and 1/4d
per pound in the winter; some of the poorer families had to
manage on just ½lb for a week. Eggs from the local farms and
smallholdings sold at ½d each. Amongst the other items on
sale in the shop were cloam pots and containers in a variety
of shapes and sizes, which were brought in by the trading
ships from Newquay and sold for a few pence each.

Above the shop were offices, a 'bank' which dealt with
the financial affairs of the coal, and other businesses
associated with the trading ships. Behind Guy's shop was a
small dressmaker and drapery store owned by a Mrs. Stephens
and her son, Samuel. Later they ran their business from a
premises in Fore Street, now the Port Isaac Stores. The
village butcher worked on Church Hill, where he had his own
slaughterhouse to which villagers would bring their livestock.
A pound of beefsteak cost just 8d (about 3p). The village
miller, Mr. Udy, had a shop in Middle Street next to what is
now the Harbour Cafe. Every morning he could be seen walking
down the valley from the mill, leading his donkey laden with
the bread and yeast buns for the shop. His two daughters
served in the shop, where ground maize and barley could also
be purchased. Later the Sherratts were to run a bakery from
what is now the Wheelhouse Restaurant. Opposite the miller's
shop was a small shop which sold boots and shoes; a good pair
of shoes cost about five shillings. The village blacksmith
was a man called Hamley; his smithy stood at the top of the
village, near to where the church rooms stand today, but he
and his wife lived in a cottage in Fore Street.

So the little community nestled around the harbour, in
so many ways self-sufficient and independent. Port Isaac
seemed to have all it needed; but one thing was more
important to it than any other: the fishing industry.
Although the trading ships moored frequently at Port Gaverne,
only the coal boats came regularly to Port Isaac, where they
never overshadowed the activities of the fishermen. Together
the two villages contained a number of small seines including
the 'Fox', the 'Providence', the 'Industry', the 'Good Intent',
the 'Mary', the 'Caroline', the 'Harlyn', the 'Rashleigh', the
'Liberty', the 'Venus' and the 'Union'. In the 1850s there
were some 49 fishing boats at Port Isaac with crews totalling
160 men; and although this number declined over the years, by
the end of the century there was still a sizeable fleet, and
it was possible to walk across the harbour on the decks of the
fishing craft. Large fishing nets could be seen hanging out
to dry from virtually every cottage in the village, and floats,
pots and other tackle lay by the doorsteps. The fishing nets

Loading slate at Port Gaverne, about 1880

Two rowing gigs pilot a large vessel past Castle Rock, about 1878.

16

had to be 'barked', i.e., coated with preservative, before
they were used; the village boasted two bark houses. One was
in Guy's yard on Roscarrock Hill, where there were large
copper furnaces used to boil up the brew — local children used
to roast potatoes in the ashes. The other bark house stood in
Dolphin Street, opposite the Dolphin Inn.

Fishing now dominated the village. Nearly every family
took an interest in it, and many people's livelihood depended
upon it; at one and the same time it brought a sense of
urgency and purpose to the community. Often the little
flotilla of boats would return home late into the summer
nights, and as it entered the harbour the piles of fish on
board shone in the moonlight. On such a night the village was
a hive of activity; lamps shone from nearly every cottage and
the doors stood open as people milled about by the Platt
waiting for the catch to be unloaded. Horses and carts were
drawn up by the fish-cellars as the fishermen carried the
baskets of fish up the beach. Children ran down to help with
the unloading, whilst the women came down to the beach with
cups of hot soup or tea for the men. As soon as the catch was
assembled the men would shout "Serve 'ee here", and the sale
would commence there and then. Sometimes in the poor lamp-
light a sovereign or half-sovereign would drop unnoticed on to
the sand, where it would be found by children playing on the
beach the next day.

The fishermen often worked in small groups or syndicates,
meeting at the end of the week to share out their profits. If
there was insufficient room in their cottages for such
business transactions, the men would meet elsewhere. One
group of four met in an upstairs room at the Dolphin Inn
(which stood in Dolphin Street, close to Temple Bar). If
there was an odd shilling left over each man took 3d worth of
brandy home to his wife for the decanter. Of course, not all
the Port Isaac fishermen sold their catch; some who had jobs
on the cargo ships during the winter would fish in the summer
months simply to provide for themselves. In such cases, the
children of the family often got the job of counting the
number of fish caught before the catch was salted down.

Herrings were kippered at the fish cellars in Port Isaac
and as they were smoked over huge fires the smoke would drift
up Church Hill and hang over the cottages. A portion of the
mackerel and pilchards caught were put to one side, ready to
be 'salted down' for the winter. It was mainly women and
young girls who were employed to do the salting down, during
which process the fish were piled upon layers of salt and left
to dry out for about a month. There was a large salting house
at Port Gaverne.

In some years, for example in 1830, there were very few

pilchards off the coast; even in a good year the season was short, from mid-July to October. Not surprisingly, fishing concerns failed from time to time, and were sold up. The 'Mary' seine at Port Isaac was sold at Mevagissey in 1816, and on April 19th 1831, the same seine was offered together with all its salt and equipment at an auction at the Port Isaac cellars. Frequently the auction of local seines took place in the Golden Lion Inn in Fore Street; the 'Liberty' seine was sold there in 1825, and the 'Industry' seine in 1840. At the end of the fishing season the Port Isaac men would take their boats over to Padstow to be laid up for the winter.

One way or another, most of the men of the village owed their employment to the sea, either as fishermen or as crew-men on the traders. If there was no work locally they would walk along the cliff paths and seek jobs at other ports. One man who did this was John Lovell Brown who, at the age of twelve, joined his first vessel, a slate trader under Captain Calloway, at Trebarwith Strand. Then, as now, some of the villagers worked as fish vendors, collecting the fish from the Platt and selling them in the inland villages around Port Isaac. Liza Bate made her living in this way; she used a donkey and trap to travel around the hamlets and villages. Donkey and cart was also the means of transport employed by a number of villagers, including a couple who lived on Church Hill and who used to ride over to Rock to harvest cockles which they then sold at 1d per pint. In 1872 two brothers, William and John Sweet, went over to Port Quin to collect mussels to sell; on the beach they were swept over by a sudden wave, and John was drowned instantly.

For some men the coastguard and lifeboat services provided employment. A retired coxswain and coastguard, William Corkhill, lived in Port Isaac for many years. In 1864 he had been coxswain on Newquay's first lifeboat, and later he was coxswain at Padstow. He was awarded a silver medal for his work in rescuing seven people from the 'Viking' which was in trouble off Harlyn Bay on April 2nd 1872, and he was awarded another medal for gallant services on March 3rd 1875. He and his wife and their daughter, Lavender, lived near the Wesleyan Chapel. William Corkhill died in 1922, but his daughter continued to live in the village, where she taught art and music.

The loading and unloading of the trading ships was generally done by casual labour; it was possible for Warwick Guy to go down on to Port Gaverne beach and hire men and women on the spot. Often such impromptu labour was rewarded, not with money, but with tokens exchangeable at Guy's shop in Port Isaac. The loading of the slate vessels was usually done by women.

Mr. and Mrs. William Corkhill outside their Port Isaac cottage, about 1910

Coal boat unloading at Port Isaac about 1890.

Some Port Isaac men worked full time or seasonally as labourers on the local farms; it was hard work from which they earned only ten or eleven shillings a week. To supplement their low incomes many families kept their own livestock. The Strout family on Church Hill reared ducklings which they were able to sell for a shilling each. Every day the children would go down to the harbour to gather limpets, which were boiled and fed to the ducks. At one time so many ducks were kept in the village that Middle Street became known locally as Duck Street. The versatile pig was another popular animal, and a row of pigsties was erected at the top of the village and hired out. The pigs were fattened during the late summer and then taken to the slaughter house. The meat was salted and hung up to dry; throughout the winter it was a source of hams and hog's puddings. The liver and heart were not wasted; they were boiled up together with rice to give a type of haggis. Not only meats were salted down for the winter; fresh vegetables were also preserved by salting, and then washed with plenty of soda and water prior to cooking. Rabbit was another popular and economical dish; usually eaten fresh, it was roasted under fat bacon and served with sage and onion stuffing.

The hunting of sea birds was fairly unusual, but one recorded attempt with disasterous consequences happened near Port Isaac, and is mentioned in the 'West Briton' for April 23rd 1845. Four men had rowed over from Trebarwith in the hope of shooting some sea fowl; arriving in Port Isaac they went to the Inn and stayed there until 7 p.m.. It was a squally night and they were advised to take some sand bags as ballast for their return journey. Instead they took some beer. Some of the villagers walked to the top of Fore Street to see them row back across the bay. About half way towards Tintagel the boat turned over in the rough sea. Immediately two fast sailing gigs set out from Port Isaac and two of the men were saved. The other two, Messrs. James Rounseval and Collecott were never seen again.

Despite severe drought from time to time, Port Isaac has never actually run out of water. There were a number of wells in the old village, including two on Roscarrock Hill, two near St. Peter's Church, and the main one in Middle Street. On the rare occasions of great water shortage, the iron wheel on the main pump was tied up to prevent its use, and the women from the village would take pots and pans up the valley and sit patiently by the mill stream to catch the trickle of water.

In the nineteenth century the village streets were not properly surfaced, but rather small pebbles were trodden down into the ground to make a hard core. In wet weather the roads soon became very muddy. The women and girls used to wear a special type of overshoe, called a patten, to keep their feet

*Park Villa, Trelights, the home of
Warwick Richard Guy in middle age.*

*Fernleigh House, Church Hill; Warwick Richard
Guy's house in Port Isaac.*

dry. A patten was essentially a shaped wooden platform
attached to a ring shaped iron base; it was held over the
shoe by two leather straps which were tied together with a
lace. Pattens cost just a few pence and could be bought from
the shop in Middle Street. For men, elastic-sided leather
boots, and for the women button-up boots were the fashion of
the day, and were usually reserved for wear on Sundays. The
fishermen usually wore thigh boots, and the farm workers
'naily boots' and leggings. Both types of worker occasionally
wore waist length smocks over their pullovers. The pullovers
were hand-made from worsted wool; some of the women would
charge 7s.6d to knit a fisherman's pullover. To keep out the
bitter Northerly winds some men would wear waistcoats under
their pullovers. Fishermen's socks were always knitted from
'fingering' wool, which cost just $2\frac{1}{2}$d an ounce. A wide
variety of headgear was worn, but the flat cap was probably
the most popular, and was worn by both men and women.

It was during Warwick Richard Guy's lifetime that his
family left Roscarrock Manor. His brother, Mark, offered it
for sale in 1867 and moved to Park Villa in Trelights, where
he died at the age of 51, on Friday, December 18th 1868.
Warwick Richard and his family lived at Park Villa for several
years, and Warwick's granddaughter, Gertrude Mary, was brought
up by her grandparents at the house. It was whilst living in
Park Villa that Warwick Richard wrote in a family album a
favourite poem of his entitled 'Do They Miss Me At Home?';
in time it could well have become his epitaph, for his
presence was to be missed at Port Isaac. By his late middle
age he had established a dominating position in the village,
and it seems fitting that he moved from Trelights into the
very centre of Port Isaac. His new and, as it turned out,
last home was Fernleigh House, which stands opposite the site
of his old shop, and at the foot of Church Hill. Fernleigh
House used to be fronted by a small garden and high iron
railings with a large gate.

It is not always easy today to realise what an important
road Church Hill was in Victorian Port Isaac. It was then the
only road into the village from Wadebridge, and was a very
busy thoroughfare. It was also quite literally the hill up to
the parish church, and funeral processions had to negotiate
this steep road. Surprisingly this led to a particularly
touching form of ceremony in which the coffins were borne
slowly up the hill by teams of bearers, whilst the mourners
followed behind singing hymns. It was a simple but very
peaceful and dignified way to leave Port Isaac.

Always the bottom of Church Hill and the Platt were
noisy and bustling; there was the coming and going of the
horses and carts, the repairing of tackle, the painting of
boats and the work of the fish cellars. Perhaps noisiest of

Coal being unloaded by shute from 'The Telegraph'. Port Isaac about 1900.

Port Isaac about 1895. Opposite the church can be seen one of the village pumps. Towards the headland, on what is today a footpath, is an old boatbuilding yard.

WARWI

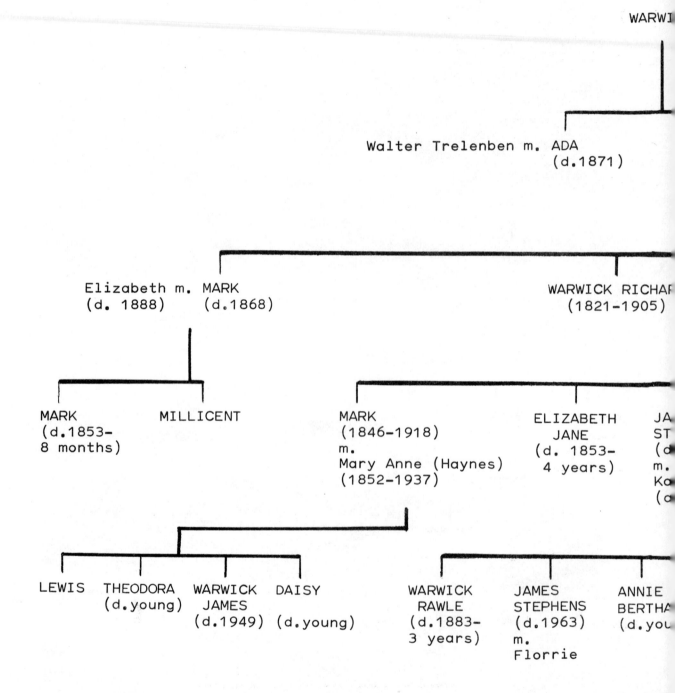

Walter Trelenben m. ADA
(d.1871)

Elizabeth m. MARK
(d. 1888)   (d.1868)

WARWICK RICHAR
(1821-1905)

MARK
(d.1853-
8 months)

MILLICENT

MARK
(1846-1918)
m.
Mary Anne (Haynes)
(1852-1937)

ELIZABETH
JANE
(d. 1853-
4 years)

JA
ST
(d
m.
Ka
(a

LEWIS

THEODORA
(d.young)

WARWICK
JAMES
(d.1949)

DAISY

(d.young)

WARWICK
RAWLE
(d.1883-
3 years)

JAMES
STEPHENS
(d.1963)
m.
Florrie

ANNIE
BERTHA
(d.you

amily

.1819)

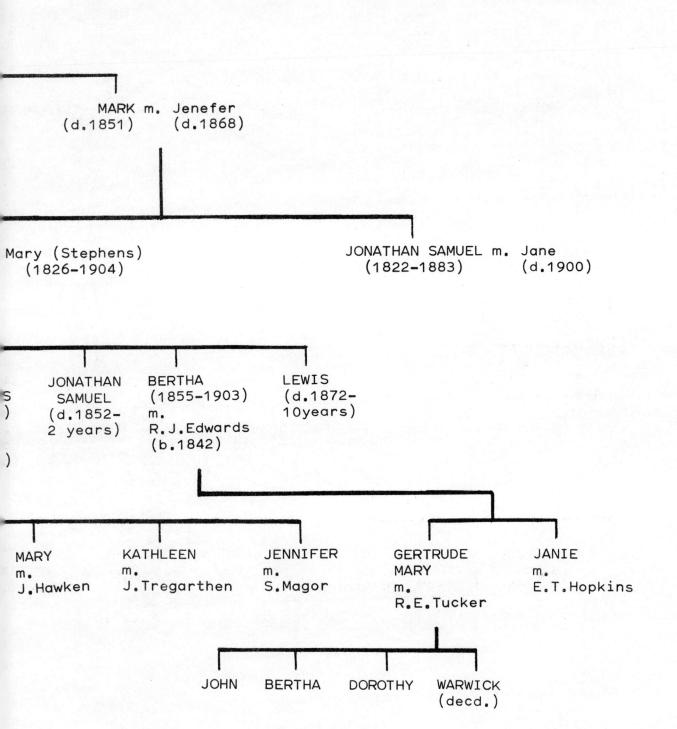

MARK m. Jenefer
(d.1851)   (d.1868)

Mary (Stephens)   JONATHAN SAMUEL m. Jane
(1826-1904)   (1822-1883)   (d.1900)

JONATHAN   BERTHA   LEWIS
S   SAMUEL   (1855-1903)   (d.1872-
)   (d.1852-   m.   10years)
           2 years)   R.J.Edwards
                         (b.1842)
)

MARY   KATHLEEN   JENNIFER   GERTRUDE   JANIE
m.   m.   m.   MARY   m.
J.Hawken   J.Tregarthen   S.Magor   m.   E.T.Hopkins
                                              R.E.Tucker

JOHN   BERTHA   DOROTHY   WARWICK
                             (decd.)

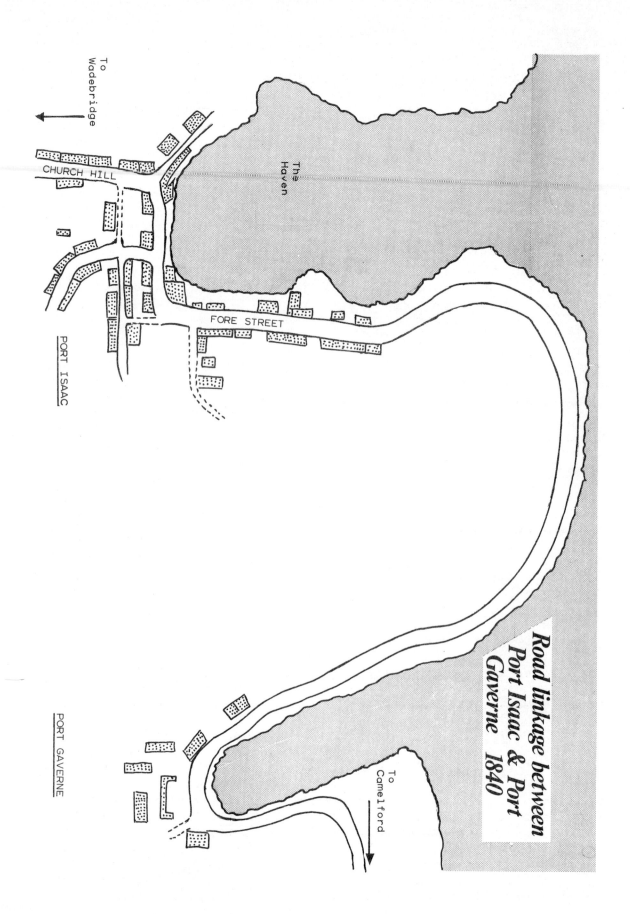

To Wadebridge

CHURCH HILL

The Haven

PORT ISAAC

FORE STREET

Road linkage between Port Isaac & Port Gaverne 1840

To Camelford

PORT GAVERNE

all were the children. Many of the fishing families had as
many as six or seven youngsters, who when they were old enough
played in the streets at the bottom of the village. The young
boys used to organise hoop races and run up and down Middle
Street and around by the Platt. The noise of the iron hoops
on the roads would irritate some of the older folk, and one
old fisherman, Thomas Hills, who lived next door to Fernleigh
House, was often seen standing in his doorway scolding the
noisy youngsters. The children often played on the beach;
skipping ropes were amongst the most popular toys. Little
boys used to try and get hold of big old sweet tins which they
made into model lifeboats to float in the harbour or on the
mill pond. No doubt, too, they admired and tried to emulate
the Cornish wrestlers of the village. Port Isaac was never
greatly renowned for its wrestling tradition, but there were
always a few enthusiasts in the village: amongst them were
Jack Glover, Samuel Bunt and Jack Thomas.

        The little girls used to play a game called 'Five
Stones', using a marble and four pebbles from the beach. The
marble was flicked up into the air and before it fell the
player had to try to pick up the four pebbles. A modern
equivalent of this game is still played today. On Saturday
afternoons the men used to take the children up the valley to
the mill pond to sail model boats. Some men used to build
model yachts of three to four feet in length with detailed
rigging and sails, and race them against each other.

        In the mid-nineteenth century Port Isaac always held a
Holiday Fair on Holy Thursday. Visiting fairs were always
very popular with the children, who would run to the top of
the hill to see them approach, and would put their ears to the
ground to hear the distant rumblings of the caravan wheels.
The fairs were held down on the Platt, usually arriving on a
Thursday and leaving on the Saturday. The entertainments
included swings, roundabouts, organ music, and dancers. The
little girls would buy wooden rings for 1d, and tiny wooden
dolls for 2d, whilst the boys would be particularly
fascinated by the displays of mechanical toys. A Mr.Flanagan
used to make model windmills to sell, and there were also
model trains and trucks which ran along a small track.

        At Port Gaverne was a lime kiln, run by Theophilus
Phillips; it provided, amongst other things, white-wash for
the cottages and fertiliser. The children from Port Isaac
used to run over to the kiln with potatoes to bake in the
ashes; a common and rather dangerous practice in Cornwall.
At Portloe in 1841 a five year old girl was burnt to death
whilst trying to take a potato from a kiln. Naturally, the
local children were brought up in the customs and traditions
of Port Isaac, and were told all the local legends. Two
stories are still quoted today. One tells of a magical crock
of gold buried somewhere at Trewetha, and the other of a

Beach huts at Port Gaverne owned by Katie Philp, about 1918. A Mrs. Mitchell owned the small teashop, which is still a cafe today,

The Slipway Restaurant, Port Isaac, formerly W. R. Guy's general stores and chandlery.

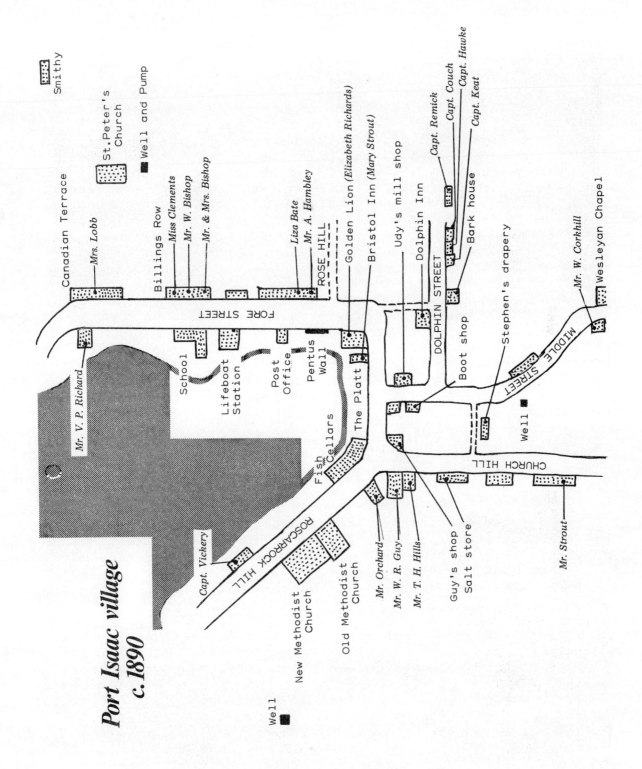

Port Isaac village c.1890

Smithy

St.Peter's Church

Well and Pump

Canadian Terrace

Mrs. Lobb

Billings Row

Miss Clements

Mr. W. Bishop

Mr. & Mrs. Bishop

Liza Bate

Mr. A. Hambley

ROSE HILL

Golden Lion (Elizabeth Richards)

Bristol Inn (Mary Strout)

Udy's mill shop

Dolphin Inn

Capt. Remick

Capt. Couch

Capt. Hawke

Capt. Keat

Bark house

Stephen's drapery

Mr. W. Corkhill

Wesleyan Chapel

DOLPHIN STREET

MIDDLE STREET

Boot shop

Well

FORE STREET

School

Lifeboat Station

Post Office

Pentus Wall

The Platt

Fish Cellars

Mr. V. P. Richard

Capt. Vickery

ROSCARROCK HILL

New Methodist Church

Old Methodist Church

Mr. Orchard

Mr. W. R. Guy

Mr. T. H. Hills

Guy's shop

Salt store

CHURCH HILL

Mr. Strout

Well

29

secret burial chamber on Roscarrock Hill, where a number of armed soldiers lie in readiness to rise and defend Cornwall against invasion. It is difficult now to know just how seriously these stories were first told; but a writer to a Cornish newspaper in 1864 wrote, "There are many in this country who still retain a belief in witchcraft. I was in company with a man a few days ago whose son had met with an accident. He told me he believed his son was overlooked, it was useless for me to try to convince him of his mistake."

In 1877 the village school was built at the cost of £2,400. Now, a hundred years later, it is about to be closed down and replaced by a new building at the top of the village. The school, standing as it did near the middle of Fore Street, added to the noise and bustle of the village. Over a hundred children in all attended, with some coming from Treore, Tresungers and Trelights, as well as from Port Gaverne and Port Quin. The school bell was rung before morning lessons began, and to avoid being late some children would come rushing down Church Hill, run across the beach and clamber up the cliff to the playing yard. In the late eighteen-hundreds (until 1891, when schooling was made free) the school charged 6d a week. It was run by a Miss Steer, and later by a Mr. Martyn; but the children acted as monitors also, to help each other. When the older ones could read and write, they taught the infants with their alphabet. The children of some of the larger and poorer families sometimes had to share their clothes and shoes, and so had to take it in turns to have a pair of shoes in which to go to school.

THE BIBLE AND THE SEA

Alphonse Esquiros in 1865 wrote of Cornwall, 'The education of the fishermen, I allow, is not very extensive. They have only studied two books, the Bible and the sea.' Today his words sound complimentary; they might well have seemed so to Warwick Richard Guy, who was himself well read in these two volumes.

Guy's childhood had a strong religious influence; his father as a boy had probably heard Wesley preach down by the Platt, and this no doubt coloured and confirmed the family's belief. In 1836 Mark Guy and Thomas Rosevear took out a long lease on two cellars at the foot of Roscarrock Hill, and a chapel was built jutting out from the hillside. By 1843 the Port Isaac Methodist Society had 102 members, and Warwick Richard was amongst them; indeed it was upon his application that the church was registered in 1846. Within a few years it was placed on the Wesleyan Model Deed, and had a regular congregation of over one hundred. Guy was one of the visiting preachers for his circuit, and he used to travel in a pony and trap to the churches in the area. He was a regular preacher at Port Quin and soon became leader of the Port Isaac Methodist Society. As Society leader his tasks were many and varied. We learn from the trustees' Minutes that on one occasion he was formally asked to go and see one member of the congregation, and attempt to make him refrain from shouting out aloud during the services. In 1865, under Guy's leadership, the decision was made to build a new church to accommodate the growing congregation. The land for the new church, which adjoined the old one, was bought from James Stephens for £100. With completion of the new church in 1869 the Society went from strength to strength. Sunday services were held at 11 a.m. and 6 p.m., with the latter so well attended that it was often necessary to arrive half an hour early in order to get a seat. A large number of the village children attended the 10 a.m. Sunday School which was held in the old church building. Guy was by now an established member of the community, and he always sat in the same side pew, wearing his fine clothes and carrying his silk top hat: he looked every inch the Victorian 'capitalist' amongst the fishermen. The inside of the church was simple and rather sombre; the women would sit on one side and the men on the other. The front and central pews had end doors and these were pay seats; a bench rent of 3 shillings a year was charged, with the money going towards the upkeep of the church. The remaining seats were free. The building was lit by a number of small oil lamps, some on poles in the gallery, and some projecting from underneath it. These lamps were also used to heat the church during the winter; in this case they were lit as early as 6.30 a.m. for the morning service, and refilled and relit again after lunch for the evening service.

Before the installation of the organ in 1920, a harmonium was used for the hymns. It stood just in front of the pulpit and was encircled by red beige curtains. For some years a Mrs. Parsons played the harmonium, while Mr. Parsons played a violin. Many of the congregation could not read or write, but they learnt their favourite hymns by heart.

The visiting preachers included a Mr. Blake from Delabole, renowned for his long sermons, and two brothers from St. Mabyn, one of whom was so short that members of the congregation had to lift him on to his horse after the service. Of course, Warwick Richard Guy talked to his family about the churches and chapels he visited; and on one occasion the maid took Guy's little granddaughter, Gertrude Mary, to a service at Port Quin. The chapel (of which nothing remains today) stood at the end of the village, but on this day it was not used. The preacher arrived upon a great white horse, and decided that because it was such a lovely day they would hold their service upon the beach. When she grew up Gertrude Mary was to share her grandfather's interest in the Roscarrock Hill church; she was organist there for many years, and her daughter is the organist today.

The Anglican church, St. Peter's, was built in the village as a 'chapel of ease' of St. Endellion parish, in the years 1882-1884 at a cost of £1,771.

The Methodist Sunday School ran one of the two temperance societies in the village. There were annual Band of Hope parades and marches, in which standards and banners were carried in procession up Fore Street. The other temperance group, which built the present social hall in Trewetha Lane, raised money from a variety of events; once they held a concert on Port Gaverne beach.

A Rechabite club also flourished in Port Isaac. Once it organised an outing to Lanhydrock House. The two-horse bus left the village at 5 a.m. on its uncomfortable journey: at every hill, up or down, the passengers had to get down and walk alongside the bus.

The village had its own daily horse-bus service to Wadebridge which was run by the Prout family. Passengers had to walk to the top of Church Hill to board the bus, which left at 9.30 a.m. It returned at about 4 p.m. and the return fare was 1s.3d. For longer journeys the Pioneer Coach, run by the North Cornwall Coach Company, operated as late as 1912 on its route through Wadebridge and Camelford to Launceston.

OLD AGE

As the nineteenth century drew to a close, the century that had seen Wellington's victory at Waterloo, the American Civil War, and the inventions of the telephone and petrol engine, Warwick Richard Guy was an old man. He, his family and his housekeeper continued to live at Fernleigh House, where the white-haired and portly Guy imposed his often eccentric will on the household. Close to the front door was a small table, on which was always a threaded needle; this was used to sew together the pages of the newspaper before it was taken to the old man.

Nevertheless, Warwick Richard's life had not been without its share of more serious worries. He had seen three of his children, Elizabeth Jane, Jonathan Samuel, and Lewis, die in early childhood. They are buried under a single headstone at St. Endellion, and their deaths offer us a startling reminder that in the mid-nineteen hundreds high rates of infant mortality haunted even the well-to-do families.

Mark Guy of Port Gaverne as a young man, about 1870.

James Stephens Guy of Padstow, about 1880.

Another daughter, Bertha, was to die before Guy himself; but he was survived by two sons, Mark and James. The younger son, James, had become a sea-captain working on the coal ships which traded between Cardiff and Padstow; the latter being the largest port near Port Isaac. James was wise to move to Padstow, for there the shipping industry lasted much longer than at Port Gaverne. Schooners traded at Padstow until the nineteen thirties.

James had married a girl called Katie; they had a son named Warwick after his grandfather, but the child died aged only three and is buried in the family plot at St. Endellion. Katie used to sail to sea with James, and when she did so she made arrangements to leave their children with other members of the family. Their son, James Stephens Guy (he had exactly the same name as his father), became a bank manager, and continued to remain in the Padstow area.

Warwick Richard's eldest son, Mark, took over much of the property at Port Gaverne; but the tide on which his father's success had been achieved had started to ebb. In 1875 he had married Mary Anne Haynes, and they moved to Beach House at Port Gaverne. Theirs was the most imposing house in the village; outside its front door stood a pair of wooden ship's cannons. Mark owned the deeds of a number of properties at Port Gaverne that had been in the family since his grandfather's time. They included the Venus cellar (which became a carpenter's shop), the Liberty cellar, three or four cottages, the Rashleigh Seine cellar, the Union cellar, and the lime kiln.

Port Gaverne had flourished during the eighteen-fifties and sixties as a port for the slate traders; entrance and exit being easier at Port Gaverne than at Port Isaac or Port Quin. The village also boasted a little fishing community. The Brown family, whose cottage now forms part of the Port Gaverne Hotel, owned several small boats including the 'Kate' and the 'Lily', both of which were named after the owner's sisters. Other Port Gaverne boats included the 'Joan', owned by Will Avery, the 'Defender', owned by Charlie Mallett, the 'Jainnie', owned by Will and George Lobb, and the 'J.M.S.' (Joey, Matilda and Sam), owned by Joey Honey. On average these little boats had crews of three or four men, working in an identical manner to those at Port Isaac.

Port Gaverne had its own inn, the Unicorn, on the site of the present hotel, which was owned and run by Elizabeth Richards, who also ran the Golden Lion at Port Isaac. The village also had its own horse-bus service to Tintagel. Most of the villagers lived in tiny cottages in amongst the numerous cellars; because there was no water supply, many of the women would do their washing in the leat. Amongst the

'characters' of old Port Gaverne was a retired sailor, Joey
Honey; he had once been coxswain of the Port Isaac lifeboat,
and before that had worked on a Cutty Sark class clipper.

Mark Guy seemed to enjoy being the virtual landlord of
Port Gaverne. Local women were employed as domestic help at
Beach House, and on occasions carriages would bring his
friends to dine at the house. But Mark's well-being depended
upon the prosperity of the village. Even before 1895, when
the arrival of the railway at Delabole killed the slate
shipping business, the fishing industry was in decline, and
the merchant schooner trade had passed its peak in the
eighteen-eighties. Mark was soon left high and dry with
property which was fast losing its value. He ran into debt
and was forced to mortgage off part of the property; in July
1891 he even mortgaged some of the cellars to his father.
Although he borrowed from various societies, including the
Independent Order of Oddfellows, Mark could only find
temporary financial relief. However, he continued to buy
small pieces of land to add to the garden around Beach House.
In 1894 he paid two guineas for a piece of land of eighty-four
square feet, at the side of the house: his purchase being
conditional upon him keeping the 'gutter at back of house
securely fenced against sheep and cattle'.

Within ten years of Mark's death, the property at Port
Gaverne which was such a burden to him was to acquire new
value for conversion to holiday chalets and flats for the
emerging tourist trade. But for Mark this salvation was to
come too late, and the Guy family lost its grip on Port
Gaverne.

Mark had two sons, Warwick James and Lewis, both of whom
emigrated; and two daughters, both of whom died young. One
of the daughters, Theodora, a pretty girl with dark curly hair,
died of poisoning after drinking some contaminated water on
Port Gaverne beach.

For Warwick Richard in Port Isaac the loss of the
property and businesses at Port Gaverne must have been a sad
blow. He had built up a prosperous shipping firm mainly from
the trade at Port Gaverne, and might well have been justified
in imagining that he had laid the foundations of a family
business for decades to come; yet within his lifetime he saw
its near total collapse. Mark had held part shares in a
vessel called the 'Telephone', but it was too late.

In 1903 Warwick Richard's daughter, Bertha, died; within
twelve months his wife, Mary, had also passed away. Left in
the end as a figure almost beyond his time, like some giant
from a past era, Warwick himself died on the last day of April
1905. His will showed the extent of his property and

influence at Port Isaac. There were tenements at Trewetha, Homer Park, and Little Trefriock, as well as numerous cottages at Port Isaac, Fernleigh House, and the old shop premises. All was divided up. His housekeeper was not forgotten; she received an annuity of £8 a year.

For decades Warwick Richard Guy had dominated the village, for many people he had been employer, landlord, shop-keeper and preacher: a powerful combination. Now he was gone, and gone soon would be the old village he knew. Modern houses were being built in Trewetha Lane, and along the terrace over-looking Port Gaverne. Port Isaac was beginning the changes which were to result in its becoming a tourist resort.

A NEW ERA

Summer visitors had been coming to the North coast of Cornwall for some years; for example, furnished sea-side lodgings were offered at Polzeath in 1847, and the tourist boom had hit Newquay in the eighteen-sixties. But it was nearer the turn of the century that visitors first came to stay in Port Isaac. In the summer of 1895 two ladies came to stay at 'Trethoway', which was then owned by a Dr. Perkins; when they departed at the end of their holiday they left gifts of clothing for the maid. The railway brought a number of early tourists: the 236 mile journey from London to Port Isaac Road station cost 20s. 3½d (third class). At the station were horses and wagonettes waiting to convey the visitors to the village, where 'several cottages and villas afford abiding places for the wayfarer at moderate prices.' Many of the younger tourists found their way to Port Gaverne beach, where old-fashioned bathing houses were erected on the beach for the enthusiastic bathers.

The early years of the new century saw the last fatal boat accident near Port Isaac. A local boat, the 'Kindly Light', was heavily laden with pilchards when she foundered in heavy seas off Varley Head. When it was obvious that she would sink, two of the crew tied their non-swimming companion, Charlie Mitchell, to some oars and let him float upon the water. The rest of the crew, including Messrs. Oaten and Calloway, struggled ashore below Roscarrock Farm, but they died of exhaustion and exposure in the bitterly cold east wind. When the boat was late returning to port, a group of Port Isaac men, including a Mr. Steer, set out along the cliff to look for her. They found Charlie Mitchell still alive, and the bodies of his dead colleagues which were later brought back to the village in a horse and cart.

Another much talked about wreck at this time was the

Wreck of the French Schooner 'Madeleine' aground in Port Quin about 1906. Local people from Port Isaac walked over the cliffs on Sunday afternoons to view the wreck.

The Venus (left) and Liberty cellars at Port Gaverne, about 1905. Note the horse drawn cart.

French schooner, 'Madeleine', which ran aground at Port Quin.
On a very high tide she was swept over the 'Cow and Calf', two
rocks which guard the entrance to the harbour, and, unable to
get out again, she broke up on the rocks. At about the same
time, there was a more famous wreck in the Atlantic, the
'Titanic'; and on her as she went down into that icy water
was a Port Isaac man named Couch.

        After his death, Warwick Guy's ships were sold off, but
some did not survive their old owner for long. The 'Bessy
Jane', once the pride of Richard Mitchell, was written off in
1907. The 'Electric', laden with coal from Newport, was
wrecked on the Stones in 1909, and the 'Telegraph' was lost in
the same year. Neither Guy's ships nor his trading business
survive as memorials to him; but in Roscarrock Hill church
his memory is recalled in a marble wall plaque which
commemorates his 62 years of service as a preacher in the
Camelford Methodist Circuit.

        A memorial of another kind can be seen in St. Peter's
church: a stained glass window recalls the memory of Raymond
Williams of the Cornwall Regiment, 'formerly chorister and
crucifer of this church, died in India 10th June 1900 aged 22'.
Sadly it was only a taste of the terrible things to come.

                        THE GREAT WAR

        The main effect of the 1914-1918 war on Port Isaac was
that it took away nearly all the men from the village for the
years of its duration, and left the streets quiet and empty.
But there were other occasions when its reality burst in upon
the little community.

        One night in the summer of 1915 several bodies washed up
on the beach at Port Gaverne. They were found to be sailors
from the S.S.'Armenian.' Their bodies were placed in simple
wooden coffins, and taken by cart up to St. Endellion churchyard where they were buried. Today two headstones commemorate
these men. One reads, '7 sailors of the Great War ... known
unto God', and the other remembers, 'Fourth Engineer Thomas
Aitcheson ... and Sailor J. Foley'.

        The Port Isaac lifeboat was kept in the building which
is now the Post Office, well up the hill above the harbour; it
was called out on several occasions during the war. Once it
was launched very speedily, within five minutes, to go to the
aid of a French ship. The ship's crew was rescued and brought
back to the harbour: one little boy from the ship leapt
ashore and ran up the beach calling out in French, much to the
interest and amusement of the villagers. One night during the

Port Gaverne about 1910.

Roscarrock hill Methodist Church as it is today. (The old chapel on the left).

war the lifeboat was being pulled down the street for a practice launch when she stuck fast on the corner by the Golden Lion. It was a rough and squally night, and some of the villagers thought that the boat was really on its way to help a ship; they hung out of their cottage windows and cried out that they could hear the screams of the drowning sailors.

The Great War took away some men from Port Isaac forever. Under a granite cross at the top of the village can be found the names of those men who never returned: F. Bate, E. Bishop, W.J. Blake, R.M. Bradshaw, C. Curtis, R. Curtis, J.B. Haynes, T. Hill, R. Hocking, G. Honey, W. Honey, A. Lark, R. Lark, J.R. Lobb, A. Masters, R. Masters, C.V. Mitchell, E. Mitchell, T.C. Mitchell, T. Mutton, T. Oaten, W. Oaten, C. Prout, E. Prout, W.E.B. Philips, I. Remick, S. Remick, R. Saundry and S. Worden. Memorials to two of these men are also to be found in Roscarrock Methodist church, and from them we learn that Richard Lobb was just 21, and Cyril Prout 19, when they died.

Richard Bradshaw had emigrated to Australia before the war, and found himself fighting in the Australian forces in France, where he was killed. His sister, Ruth, continued to live in Port Isaac; and at her request a fellow Port Isaac soldier, Samuel Bunt, who served in the army of occupation after 1918, visited her brother's grave. At the end of the war the village celebrated with a carnival; but the joy was short-lived, for many of the men who returned could not find employment. Horse-drawn wagons used to come down to Port Gaverne to take them up to sign on at the labour exchange in Camelford.

Mark Guy died on December 7th 1918, three days before his seventy-second birthday. After considerable dealings his estate was wound up; for the first time in a hundred years the Guy family were not major land owners at Port Gaverne. The Liberty cellars, together with the adjacent house and gardens, were conveyed to Rosina Ashton, who soon set about converting them to living accommodation. It was particularly difficult to dry out the walls of the old salt stores.

The mood of the villagers in Port Gaverne and Port Isaac was optimistic; they had a new industry, tourism, which showed every sign of growing up to replace trading and fishing. As elsewhere, the Great War had been a social watershed, and things could never again be the same.

POSTSCRIPT

When this story started with the yeoman Warwick Guy of St. Endellion, George III was still King; the end is now

Church Hill, Port Isaac, as it is today.

A recent view of Port Isaac. Fernleigh House (left) at bottom of Church Hill, Roscarrock Chapel in centre.

reached with George V on the throne and David Lloyd George as Prime Minister. In recounting the life of Warwick Richard Guy we have traversed the reigns of five monarchs, and through it all have snatched a brief glimpse of life at the high tide of Port Isaac's history.

APPENDIX A

SHIPS OWNED BY MR. WARWICK RICHARD GUY

NAME	BUILT	DATE	TONNAGE	MASTS	LENGTH (feet)
'Bessy Jane'	Port Isaac	1850	57	2	59
'Sylph'	Port Isaac	1853	38	1	52
'Agenoria'	Port Gaverne	1858	?	2	77
'Agenova'	Port Gaverne	1858	49	1	59
'Telegraph'	Port Gaverne	1859	41	1	55
'Volunteer'	Port Gaverne	1861	?	?	?
'Electric'	Port Gaverne	1863	48	1	58
'Surprise'	Port Gaverne	1879	?	2	59
'Ida' *	?	?	155	?	?

*Listed as belonging to Warwick R. Guy of Port Isaac
...'Lloyds Register Steamers 1907-8'

Some of these vessels were held in co-ownership: The 'Agenoria' was owned together with Messrs. John Neal and J. Hawk, the 'Electric' together with Messrs. Joseph Waters and Job Hockaday, the 'Volunteer' by Guy and S. Phillips, the 'Bessy Jane' together with Messrs. James Stephens and James Bate, and the 'Sylph' by Guy and Thomas Mitchell.

LAND AROUND PORT ISAAC OWNED BY THE GUY FAMILY (1840)
(Taken from a Rate Book of that time.)

Occupier of the land	Owner	Description of property
Thomas Brown	Warwick Guy	house/garden at Trelights
Mark Burton	Mark Guy	house at Port Quin
Mary Blake	Mark Guy	house at Port Quin
William Brown	Mark Guy	house at Port Quin
Sophia Bishop	Mark Guy	house at Port Quin
William Bragg	Mark Guy	house/garden at Port Isaac
John Chalk	Mark Guy	house/garden at Port Quin
Grace Cock	Mark Guy	house/garden at Port Quin
John Ellery	Mark Guy	house at Port Quin
Samuel Ellery	Mark Guy	house at Port Quin
Thomas George	Mark Guy	house/garden at Port Quin
Jonathan Guy	himself	Treswarrow, Trelights
Jonathan Guy	himself	Treswarrow Park
Warwick Guy	himself	land at Burrow Park
Warwick Guy	himself	land at Trewethick Park
Warwick Guy	Hon.A.M.Agar	Agar's Park
Warwick Guy	Samuel Cleave	Land's Park
Warwick Guy	Hon.A.M.Agar	Trecrege Park, Trelights
Warwick Guy	Executors of Samuel Billings	Pawley's Park
Mark Guy	himself	Roscarrock Park
Mark Guy	himself	Trewint Park
Mark Guy	himself	Kearn's Park
Mark Guy	himself	Cornish's Park
Mark Guy	himself	Archers, Trewetha
Mark Guy	himself	Union cellar (Port Gaverne)
Mark Guy	himself	sand pit at Port Isaac
Mark Guy	himself	cellar at Port Isaac
Mark Guy	Anne Richards	cellar at Port Isaac
Mark Guy	Mr. Lyne	land at Bodannon
John Hawke	Mark Guy	Mill and garden at Port Quin
F.B.Hamley	Mark Guy	fishcellars Rashleigh, Venus
John Iles	Mark Guy	house at Port Quin
John Kellow	Warwick Guy	house/garden at Trelights
William Long	Mark Guy	garden at Port Quin
Honor Martyn	Mark Guy	house at Port Isaac
Theophilus Phillips	Mark Guy	limekiln at Port Gaverne
John Phillips	Mark Guy	house at Port Quin
John Prout	Mark Guy	house at Port Quin
John Phillip	Mark Guy	house at Port Quin
Richard Phillip	Mark Guy	house at Port Quin
Thomas Skinner	Mark Guy	house/garden at Port Isaac
John Tamblyn	Mark Guy	house at Port Isaac
William Thomas	Mark Guy	house/garden at Port Isaac
John Thomas	Mark Guy	house at Port Isaac
John Thomas	Warwick Guy	house/garden at Trelights

APPENDIX C

GUY FAMILY MARRIAGES AT ST. ENDELLION: 1698 - 1810

THOMAS GUY and Mary Smyth	August 6th 1698
BARBARA GUY and William Brown	September 22nd 1698
THOMAS GUY and Anne Williams	November 11th 1700
RICHARD GUY and Catherine Lark	November 24th 1710
MARY GUY and Mark Bishop	January 2nd 1713
AMBROS GUY and Mary Lang	October 21st 1722
JOAN GUY and Abraham Hicks	June 12th 1729
WILLIAM GUY and Elizabeth Phillip	June 30th 1731
MARY GUY and William Skinner	February 14th 1736
AMBROSE GUY and Elizabeth Steer	September 19th 1737
MARK GUY and Joan Kent	October 1st 1740
ANTONY GUY and Katherine Kent	May 4th 1741
THOMAS GUY and Grace Jagoe	October 3rd 1742
ANN GUY and Clement Kendall	March 27th 1744
ELIZABETH GUY and Thomas Knight	November 9th 1751
GEORGE GUY and Mary Trevithick	February 14th 1753
MARK GUY and Ann Gray (lic)	December 21st 1753
WILLIAM GUY and Elizabeth May (lic)	June 8th 1755
ANNE GUY and Thomas Tonking of St.Kew	June 29th 1755
CATHERINE GUY and John Sparnall	October 23rd 1757
JONATHAN GUY and Elizabeth Henderson	February 7th 1764
JOHN GUY and Prudence Gath (lic)	August 27th 1767
ANTHONY GUY and Mary Buller	July 19th 1768
WARWICK GUY and Grace Mallet (lic)	April 4th 1776
JOAN GUY and Richardson Gray (lic)	February 20th 1787
CATHERINE GUY and William Billing,mariner	December 10th 1792
SARAH GUY and William Billing (lic)	February 17th 1801
SARAH GUY and John Brown	May 15th 1804
GRACE GUY and Robert Pearse of Lanteglos (lic)	May 23rd 1805
JOAN GUY and Richard Caesar Cock w, (lic)	April 16th 1807
MARK GUY and Elizabeth George (lic)	June 20th 1809
CATHERINE GUY and Samuel Worden (lic)	March 5th 1810

BIBLIOGRAPHY

THE MERCHANT SCHOONERS.   B.Greenhill.   David & Charles, 1968

A HISTORY OF CORNISH MAIL AND STAGE COACHES.   C.Noall.
        D. Bradford Barton, 1963

ENGLAND'S RIVIERA.   J.Harris Stone.   Paul, Trench and Truber
        & Co., London.

BYGONE CORNWALL.   ed. J.N.Rosewarne.   D.Bradford Barton, 1970

MURRAY'S HANDBOOK FOR DEVON AND CORNWALL, 1859.   reprinted
        David & Charles, 1971

CORNISH SHIPWRECKS, VOL.II: THE NORTH COAST.   C.Carter.
        David & Charles, 1970

CORNWALL: ITS MINES AND MINERS.   J.R.Leifchild.   Frank Cass
        & Co. Ltd., 1968

CORNISH SEINES AND SEINERS.   C.Noall.   D.Bradford Barton, 1972

CORNWALL AND ITS COASTS.   A.Esquiros.   Chapman & Hall,
        London, 1865

LAKES PAROCHIAL HISTORY OF CORNWALL.   J.Polsue.   E.P.
        Publishing Ltd.

COLLECTANEA CORNUBIENSIA.   Boase.   1890

METHODISM IN THE CAMELFORD AND WADEBRIDGE CIRCUIT, 1743-1963.
        T.Shaw.   1964

NEW BRITISH TRAVELLER. VOL.I: CORNWALL.   Dugdale

CORNWALL. S.Baring-Gould.   Cambridge University Press, 1910

HISTORY OF CORNWALL. VOL.II.   F.Hitchens and S.Drew

AN ILLUSTRATED ITINERARY OF CORNWALL.   C.Redding.   1842

KELLY'S DIRECTORY for 1923

LODENEK PRESS PADSTOW

Onen Hag Oll

The Lodenek Press issues Cornish books of authority, and is dedicated to the belief that behind the so-called facade of 'Vanishing Cornwall' lies a way of life that is still valid and vigorous. Among the books we have published are:—

THE STORY OF PORT ISAAC, PORT QUIN AND PORT GAVERNE, by Monica
Winstanley

PADSTOW'S OBBY OSS AND MAY DAY FESTIVITIES, by Donald R. Rawe.

HURLING AT ST. COLUMB AND IN CORNWALL, by A. Ivan Rabey.

NAMES FOR THE CORNISH, 300 Cornish Christian Names, by Christopher Bice.

CORNISH DIALECT AND FOLK SONGS, collected by Ralph Dunstan.

THE CORNISH SONG BOOK Parts I and II, by Ralph Dunstan.

COUSIN JENNIE'S CORNISH COOK BOOK, by Pamela Pascoe.

and The CORNISH PLAYS SERIES

Send for full list of publications, supplied free.

Warwick Richard Guy about 1870